Quantifying Chaos: The Science of Neo-Anarchism

Henry Kirchhoff

Chapter I: Basic Principles

The definition of chaos and order requires first consideration of the phenomena which influence them:

1. The frames in which both operate.
2. Perpetuates and inhibitors of chaos and order

The first frame in which chaos and order operate is time. In this paradigm pure order (total stability) situates itself in diametric opposition to pure chaos (constant change). Their relationship is best visualized as a gradient which moves from pure order to neutrality, and then from neutrality to pure chaos:

Pure Order	Predominant Order	Neutral
\/	\/	\/
Unchanging	Stable Change	Neutral

Neutral	Predominant Chaos	Pure Chaos
\/	\/	\/
Neutral	Unstable Change	Constant Change

The second frame in which chaos and order manifest is space. In the spatial frame pure order manifests as stable creation whereas pure chaos manifests as unstable destruction. Their relationship manifests as follows:

Pure Order	Predominant Order	Neutral
\/	\/	\/
Stable Creation	Stable Destruction	Neutral

Neutral	Predominant Chaos	Pure Chaos
\/	\/	\/
Neutral	Unstable Creation	Unstable Destruction

Destruction

Order   Change
1   D
V   V   V

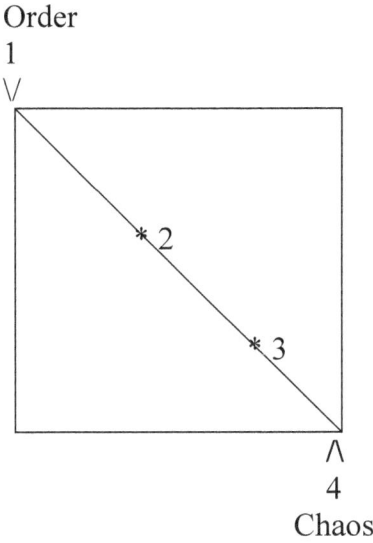

Fig. 3
System Scale

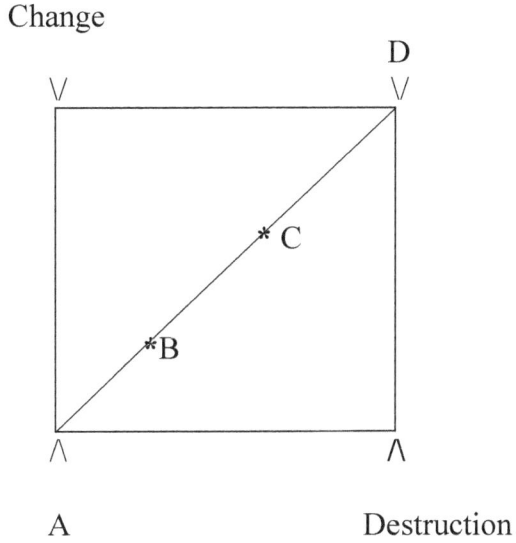

Fig. 4
Scale Perpetuate

In Fig. 4, "A" represents the amount of change destruction has caused in a closed system (currently 0). Point "1" in Fig. 3 represents the initial relationship between order and chaos before the system perpetuate begins to take effect, pure order predominating.

The relationship between the system perpetuate, in this case destruction, and the system scale, is such that the destructive energy plus entropy equals product on the system scale:

(destructive energy + entropy = product on c & o scale)

Entropy is a primary variable in determining the effect of a system perpetuate on the chaos and order scale. This is because entropy contributes to the increase of disorder[2] in the universe, a state which is arguably irreversible. Entropy in itself represents the degradation of energy from a productive state to non-productive. To illustrate both this and entropy's irreversible nature, a common example is used: the

---

[2] The believed correlation between entropy and disorder is under debate.

combination of dye and water. In a closed system dye and water will mix, and can never be separated. The energy used to equally distribute these molecules cannot be used to separate the molecules once more, nor can it be used to further mix the molecules. The energy in this system is now unable to do work.

Entropy has the potential to change the random nature of subsequent systems. Imagine three bottles in a single room opened in succession. The molecular dispersion of the first system will inhibit the molecular dispersion of the second. Likewise, the molecular dispersion of the second system will inhibit the third. When the molecular dispersion of prior systems has fully inhibited the molecular dispersion of a subsequent system, this is known as the **entropic threshold**.

If the molecular example above holds any metaphorical accuracy—the closed environment signifying the universe, the molecules signifying entropy—the universe has a capacity for useless energy, and the dispersal of this energy inhibits the dispersal of energy in other systems. The world perpetually spirals towards stagnation.

The following example illustrates entropy's basic role in quantifying chaos. For basic quantification consider both perpetuate and system scales equal to one. In addition, for simplicity assume entropy = unit movement of destruction. Next, let us say that the level of destruction in Fig. 4 moves from point A to point B, or, .25 units. In response, the scale in Fig. 3 moves from point 1 to point 3 (.5 units). Such a change illustrates a disproportionate relationship between the system perpetuate and the chaos and order scale. The Perpetuate, moving only .25 units from point A to B, causes the chaos and order scale to shift .5 units from point 1 to point 3. This is because, in addition to the chaos produced from destruction, entropy contributes to the level of chaos.

Here we have equated entropy produced with destructive energy converted such that a .25 shift in destructive energy results in .25 production of entropy. Such a precise conversion would likely never occur and is purely hypothetical to illustrate how the system perpetuate destruction works under the influence of entropy. There are minor factors and variables to be discussed later, which alter the simplified depiction of destruction.

Creation

Order
1
V

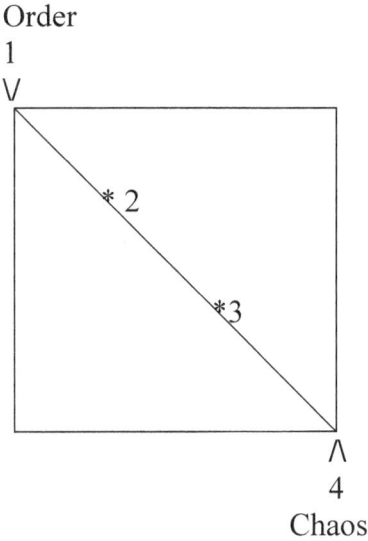

Fig. 5
System Scale

Change   D
V   V

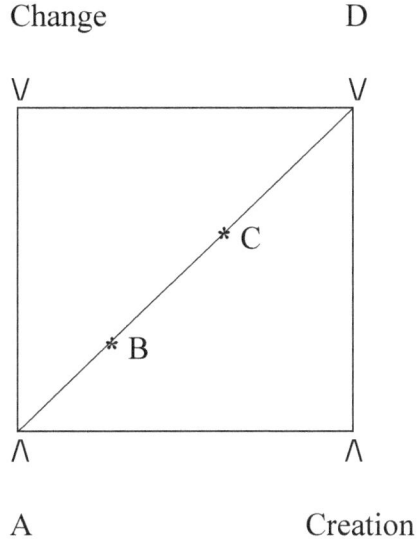

∧   ∧
Chaos   A   Creation
Fig. 6
Scale Perpetuate

The "A" in Fig. 6 represents the amount of change creation has caused in a closed system (currently 0). Point 1 in Fig. 5 represents the initial relationship between order and chaos before the system perpetuate begins to take effect.

The general relationship between the given system perpetuate: creation, and the chaos and order scale is such that the creative energy minus entropy equals product.

(creative energy - entropy = product on c & o scale)

Assuming as we did in Fig. 2 and Fig. 3, that entropy and the energy exerted are equal, a movement from point A to point B in the system perpetuate will cause zero change in the chaos and order scale. This is because, as shown in the equation above, the energy exerted is negated in this instance due to entropy.

Conversion

It is important to remember that when we speak of creation and destruction we are acknowledging that essentially only conversion exists, and that when one object or system is destroyed another object or system is effectively being created.

Therefore, when creation or destruction is referred to as an end we are referring to the active pursuit of a perpetuate in a paradigm where both occur simultaneously. For example, if destruction is actively pursued we set the perpetuate up to chart destruction despite the fact that something is inadvertently being created as a result of destruction.

When quantifying order and chaos one should take into consideration mathematically the amount of order or chaos inadvertently produced in a system. Initially, the product = total order or chaos produced. Subtract inadvertent chaos or order produced if calculable and the result will be your net product or actual product.[3]

The only time a perpetuate can change is when the byproduct of active pursuit begins to outweigh the product of active pursuit such as when destruction produces more order and stability in its wake than chaos.[4]

It is important to note a few significant things about conversion:

1. **The Law of Diminishing Returns**: the product of energy or conversion from energy to product transfers at a less than equal rate.

This is also posited in the second law of thermodynamics which states that "with each energy conversion from one form to another, a portion of the energy becomes unavailable for further use." This energy unavailable for further use is known as entropy, measured as follows:

(energy input – efficient energy output = entropy)

---

[3] See Section Stable-Constant: Chaos: Destruction Gradient to see what happens when inadvertent byproduct outweighs active pursuit

[4] This is discussed in greater detail in Chapter III, p. 22, heading **Stable-Constant: Chaos.**

Chapter II: System Models

The system scale can change at variable rates, the primary being:

1. Stable Constant
2. Stable Inconstant
3. Unstable Constant
4. Unstable Inconstant

The effects of a perpetuate and respective entropy production are variable depending on which system model they manifest in. This is because the relationship between the perpetuate, entropy, and the resulting energy can be enhanced or diminished depending on the system's stability or constancy.

Stability

Stability – Refers to the increments of time at which one unit mass or energy change occurs over a fixed period of time. Stability in this context, or **system stability**, differs from both thermodynamic and kinetic stability, both common to those acquainted with physics and/or chemistry. In chemistry, kinetic stability refers to the amount of time it takes for a reaction to transpire. Kinetic stability shares a correlative relationship with the transpiration of time. The longer the reaction takes to transpire, the greater the kinetic stability.

A chemical compound with a high kinetic stability would not necessarily have high system stability. Though the reaction might take a long time to complete its cycle, this does not necessarily mean that the reaction occurred at a stable rate, or that there were not various stages in the kinetically stable compound during which the rate of change fluctuated significantly.

Stability on the system scale differs also from chemical instability. Chemical instability refers to the tendency of a system to change drastically in nature when a variable is added to the compound. For example, nitro glycerin will explode when force is exerted on it. Chemical instability, therefore, refers to the sensitivity of a system to external forces, or a tendency towards change when external forces are applied, i.e. chemical instability refers to what could happen. System stability, on the other hand, is a means of measuring chaos composition in closed systems after the system has already undergone change or as it is undergoing change.

Thermodynamic stability refers to the amount of conversion underwent or completed when a substance reaches equilibrium; the higher the conversion, the higher the thermodynamic instability. The amount of conversion that occurs is independent of system stability as well. For example, a system could convert only a little while reaching equilibrium and have a low system stability rate, as the fluctuation in rate of conversion during the small occurrence of change was so great.

In summation: thermodynamic stability refers to a quantity of conversion, kinetic stability refers to the rate of conversion or reaction, and chaotic stability refers to not the total rate, but the incremental rate at which the conversion or reaction takes place.

Stability as a Unit of Measurement

The unit of measurement only provides a uniform means of measuring a phenomenon to facilitate to the measurement of distinction between units of change over allotted units of time. To acquire a more acute measurement of stability one may resort to measuring incremental change per minute, or incremental change per 30 seconds. Likewise, if measuring something of less weight (1gram), employing smaller increments of measurement, such as the milligram, provides more efficient and detailed information.

The Relativity of Time in Stability Measurement

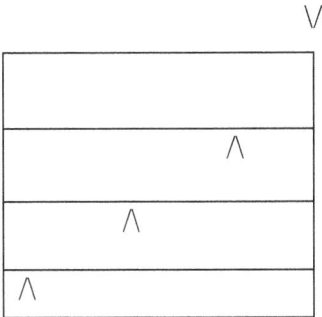

Fig. 7
Stable Change

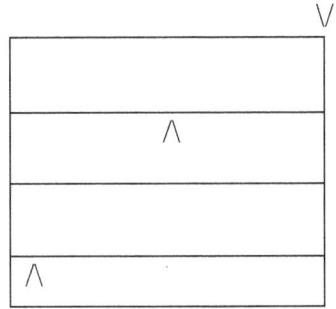

Fig. 8
Unstable Change

Fig. 7 represents stable change over a given time period. Each of the four changes takes the same amount of time. It is recognized as a **change-stage**. Due to the variable of measurement, a change-stage could effectively represent a system scale, or a system scale could be composed of several change-stages. Fig. 8 represents unstable change over the course of one change-stage. For this example we will say that the change-stage depicted in Fig. 7 and Fig. 8 occurs over the course of one minute.

In Fig. 7 the four stable increments occur at the same intervals. Over the course of the given timeframe: one minute, the stable incremental growth is occurring once every 15 seconds until it reaches the peak.

In Fig. 8, we have a much different circumstance. The incremental growth in Fig. 8 moves up two bars from the starting point, and then moves only one bar. This inconsistency over the course of one minute is referred to as unstable change. However, the nature of this seemingly inconsistent model alters significantly when we change the timeframe:

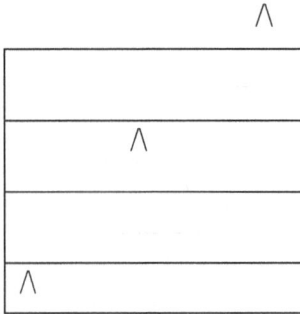

Fig. 9
Unstable, Minute 1

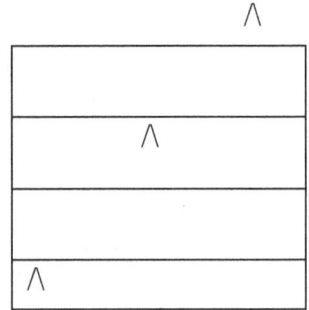

Fig. 10
Unstable, Minute 2

In Figures 9 & 10 change takes place at varying intervals. Each change-stage in itself is an example of unstable change. But if the unstable pattern continues and repeats itself over the course of a series of change-stages measured together, the repetition becomes a **relative stability**. The relative stability illustrated in the figures above becomes so due to the synonymous nature of the change stages. If this process repeats, the relative stability becomes increasingly potent. In many cases change-stages are determined after a system scale is charted. The change-stage is merely a means of quantifying relative stability and relative constancy after the system scale is charted.

Quantifying Stability

Stability refers to adherence to a stable rate of change. Instability is deviation from stable incremental growth. To determine the stable incremental growth of a system scale measure deviation or lack thereof, from the previous **revolution** of change that occurred within the system scale. Revolution refers to a full change that occurs within a system scale. For example, when converting water to steam there are two revolutions: ice to water and water to steam. To measure stability in a system where only one revolution occurs, calculate rate of change from beginning of process to the middle and from middle to end: break the revolution into change-stages.

The first full revolution that occurs within a system is always assumed to be at maximum stability. This is because all energy in the system is workable, thus entropy-barren. To determine stability measure the first subsequent revolution in the succession against the initial revolution. The rest are measured successively: revolution three against revolution two, revolution four against revolution three, etc.

Imagine that a system reaches equilibrium over the course of one minute with full revolutions occurring every ten seconds, creating a stable model. If the first revolution occurs over the course of ten seconds, subtract it from the amount of time it takes for the second revolution to complete, which in this hypothetical case results in 0. The rate of deviation therefore is 0 seconds per revolution, or, (0 sec. per revolution).

However, imagine instead that the first full revolution remaining constant, the second revolution took 20 seconds to achieve. This would result in a rate of deviation of 10 sec. per revolution. The fractional value of deviation would be 1/2, whereas decimal value would equal .5 for the two following reasons:

1. Out of two revolutions one stable and one deviation occurred.

2. Because the second revolution took twice as long, creating a positive deviation value and a negative efficiency value.

Deviation value = the amount of deviation relative to the amount of revolutions which have occurred. **Efficiency value** = an increase or decrease in the amount of time during subsequent revolutions. Increase in time means a lower efficiency value, and vice versa.

Efficiency and deviation share a negative correlative relationship when deviation occurs between the first and second revolutions. Following this, however, their relationship is harder to gauge, as efficiency must always be measured in terms of the greatest and smallest efficiency within a system whereas deviation must always be measured in terms of the preceding revolution of change.

If the third revolution lasted 20 seconds and we measured the rate of deviation against the initial revolution there would be another 50% increase in deviation when in reality there is no deviation from the preceding revolution at all. If we measure each successive revolution against the first increment, a stabilizing system could mathematically appear to be very unstable.

13

However, when we measure the third revolution against the second we see a deviation rate of 0 has occurred. Since three revolutions have occurred and only one has deviated from a prior revolution, the fractional value of deviation would be 1/3, with a decimal value nearing .334. deviation per 30 seconds. Logically, if the rate of revolution remains the same the rate of deviation will decrease likewise.

Efficiency, on the other hand, is quite different. In the above example, revolutions two and three are identical. Whereas deviation value decreases as a result of the relationship between revolutions two and three, efficiency is not affected. Efficiency only measures decrease or increase in time during which a revolution occurs. The most efficient revolution is referred to as **maximum efficiency** whereas the least efficient is referred to as **minimum efficiency**.

If a fluctuation occurs in a change-stage such that efficiency reduces and then increases again, we are merely capable of citing when the changes in efficiency occur. While deviation can be averaged (50% rate of deviation), there is no rate of efficiency. We can only make the observation that, between particular revolutions, efficiency increases, decreases, or remains stable. This is because if we tried to determine a rate of efficiency, one would not be able to derive at which points fluctuations occurred, and whether or not these fluctuations were positive or negative.

Final Value

Value is important because, once the system is complete the value determines whether the system is stable or unstable. For example, a system with ten revolutions is represented by increments graphically, and five deviations from preceding revolutions would have a final or total value of 50%, which means that a system is marked by 50% instability. A system with more than 50% deviation is predominantly unstable. A system with less than 50% deviation is predominantly stable.

Constancy

Constancy – refers to the persistence towards a given direction over a fixed period of time:

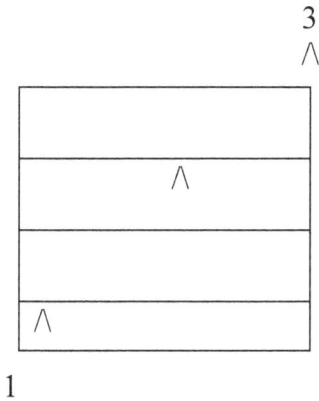

```
        3                              4
        /\                             /\
 ┌──────────────┐              ┌──────────────┐
 │              │              │              │
 │      /\      │              │      /\      │
 │              │              │              │
 ├──────────────┤              ├──────────────┤
 │              │              │         /\   │
 ├──────────────┤              ├──────────────┤
 │ /\           │              │ /\           │
 └──────────────┘              └──────────────┘
  1                             1
```

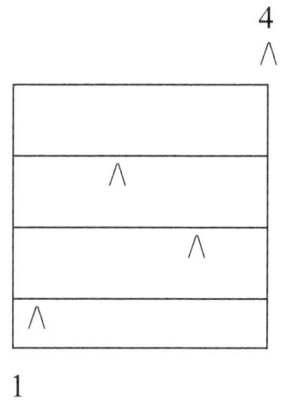

Fig. 11   **Fig. 12**
Constant   **Inconstant**

       Fig. 11 represents constant change over one change-stage. Fig. 12 represents unstable change over the course of one change-stage.

       In Fig. 11 the three increments illustrate a steady, unidirectional growth towards a uniform outcome, represented by "3" Fig. 12, on the other hand, illustrates a highly inconstant model, one in which fluctuations move both up and down the system perpetuate scale. So, though both reach the same outcome, one has achieved the means via constancy, the other via inconstancy.

       There are two instances in which inconstancy occurs. The first is when entropy from the first revolution in a system is so great that it significantly affects subsequent revolutions. The second instance is when a system that normally perpetuates chaos suddenly perpetuates order. Occasionally, such is the case using destruction as a perpetuate[5]

---

[5] This is discussed more in Chapter III, p. 24. Heading: **Stable-Constant: Chaos**

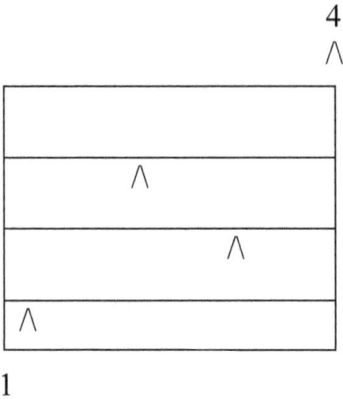

Fig. 13
Inconstant, Minute 1

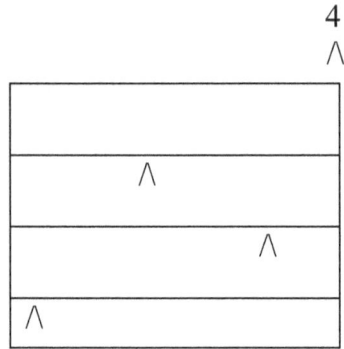

Fig. 14
Inconstant, Minute 2

In figures 13 & 14 the inconstancy repeats in the same manner as the stability models depicted in figures 9 & 10. Likewise, both figures 13 and 14 are in themselves examples of inconstant change. As with stability, if the inconstant pattern continues and repeats itself over the course of a series of changes measured together the repetition becomes a **relative constancy**. Potency of the relative constancy increases in accordance with the amount the inconstant pattern is repeated.

Measuring Constancy

Constancy is continuous motion towards a unified final output. Inconstancy is deviation from the perpetual movement towards a single output. Just as with stability, determining the constancy of a change-stage requires the measurement of deviation from the previous revolution. As with stability, the initial revolution is always assumed to be at maximum constancy.

The one significant distinction between measuring constancy and stability lies in their respective forms of deviation. Whereas stability is measured in terms of a revolution's time-deviation from a prior revolution, constancy is measured in terms of incremental movement towards or away from preferred outcome.

Say, for example, that one change-stage takes place over the course of one minute. If a feature of the system was stable incremental growth at ten seconds per revolution, but the revolutions had alternating values in terms of chaos/order production, we would have a stable-inconstant system, which would graphically manifest as follows:

Chaos
\/

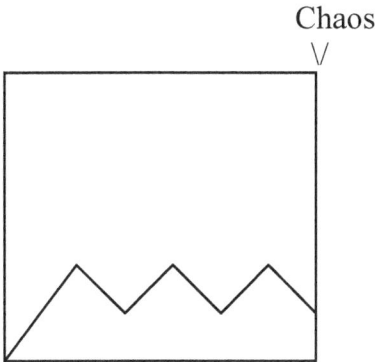

Fig. 15
Stable-Inconstant

In Fig. 15, the uprising revolutions represent movement towards the linear goal chaos. However, alternating revolutions are descending, implying that the means of perpetuating chaos is actually serving to perpetuate order.

Each of the alternating movements represents a ten second revolution. Because this model occurs over the course of one minute, we provide 60 seconds to measure deviation of stability, and 60 increments to measure constancy. Imagine that the first movement is 20 increments, whereas the alternating movement only descends 10 increments. The deviation from constancy, therefore, is 10 increments per 20 seconds. But then the third alternating movement occurs, bringing incremental growth towards chaos (constancy) back to 20 increments per 30 seconds and causing an overall constancy deviation of 10 increments per 30 sec. Any deviation marks a change in direction between two revolutions.

When incremental constancy, and deviation from are added, they should equal the incremental capacity, or, the quantity of increments one chose to measure with.

Notice the important, yet possibly erroneous underlying implication derived from the means of measuring both stability and

17

constancy, which is, since the first revolution is considered to be at maximum constancy/stability, pure inconstancy and pure instability can never truly exist.

Resulting Models

Both stability and constancy are order-based, whereas instability and inconstancy are chaos-based. Their relationships graphically manifest as follows:

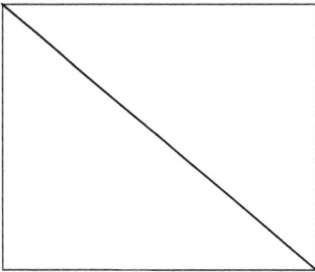

Stable Constant
Fig. 15

Stable Constant:
Characterized by incremental growth constantly moving in a uniform direction. In Fig. 15 the steady incremental growth is constantly heading towards the maximum output. Order generally thrives in this system, whereas chaos generally diminishes.

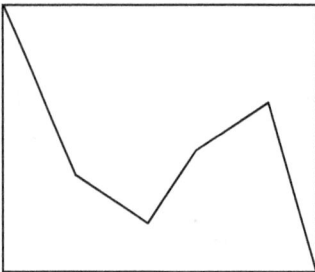

Stable Inconstant
Fig. 16

Stable Inconstant: In this model the incremental growth is stable. Each revolution takes the same amount of time to complete. Growth towards the preferred outcome, however, is not uniform. Thus far, stability and constancy are considered equal quantifications of chaos and order. Therefore, it is as of now indeterminate which works better in this system.

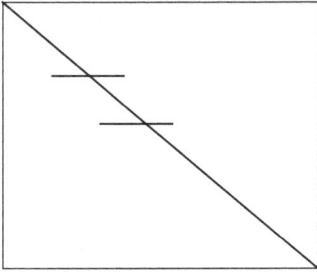

Unstable Constant
Fig. 17

Unstable Constant: The two lines intersecting the slide-scale in Fig. 17 depict the unstable revolutions. While the model is constant in that it remains fixed on a particular destination the intervals at which change occur vary greatly. Again, so far it has been determined that chaos and order are equally likely to flourish in this system.

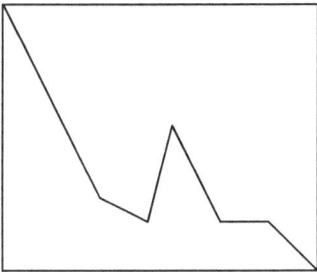

Unstable Inconstant
Fig. 18

Unstable Inconstant: Neither stable incremental growth, nor constant movement in a linear direction are present in this model, making it the ideal breeding ground for chaos.

Chapter III: Stable Change
Stable Change: Order

Stable-Constant: Order-Based

Fig. 15 depicts the first possible stable-constant system of change. If we use creation in this model to perpetuate order then we have the successful energy output, the stability, and the constancy of the system to counterbalance the entropy. Therefore:

successful energy output + stability + constancy – entropy – inadvertent chaos = product on c & o scale

For the sake of covering a broad range of possibilities in the most linear fashion, assume that change towards order via creation and eventually, total order, is the goal of this closed system. We must now look at how order can thrive with the aid of stability and constancy. Since our goal is to reach maximum or near-maximum order we shall begin at the bottom of the chaos and order system in Fig. 19.

Order

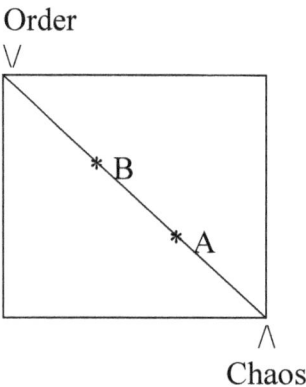

Chaos

Fig. 19

In the above diagram point "A" represents the current balance between order and chaos. In a system leaning towards chaos one of two phenomena can occur which produce order. The first is the creation of several distinctive orders.

Creating order via distinctive orders is less potent than creating order via one single force, or creating order via unification of distinctive orders. However, due to the strong correlation between stability + constancy + efficient output; entropy, and the diversity of distinctive orders, rarely outweigh the order produced and inherit in the system.

Once we reach the midpoint of the universal scale, represented by point "B," the system of perpetuating order via creation must change. If we exceed the midpoint by continuing to create new distinctive orders, the number of orders will inadvertently amass a greater amount of distinction, at which point creating more distinctive orders will actually cause creation to perpetuate chaos rather than order.

For the system to most efficiently perpetuate order from the midpoint the newly created orders must integrate into a single order. It is the only point at which pure order can exist.

Change
\/

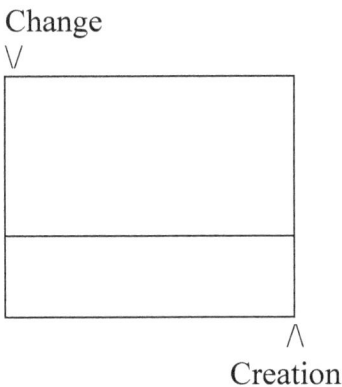

/\
Creation

Fig. 20

Fig. 20 depicts the second possible system of stable-constant change. At this time the system has no practical applications when referring to order-based systems.

Stable-Inconstant: Order-Based

Fig. 16 represents the basic stable-inconstant model, a model in which order can comfortably operate. In this instance constancy is subtracted from stability, or rather, inconstancy is added to stability, therefore:

successful energy output + stability – constancy – entropy = product on c & o scale – inadvertent chaos

The model depicted in Fig. 16 occurs if a bond between distinctive orders is created and chaos from creation of new distinctive orders is equal to the order from the bond or unification of pre-existing distinctive orders.

The first arch represents the point at which the bond and the distinctive orders reach a momentary equilibrium in which change occurs, but neither chaos nor order is generated. The third arch is the point at which order produced from the bond between distinctive orders begins to outweigh the chaos of the new distinctive orders created.

Stable Change: Chaos

Stable-Constant: Chaos

After the midpoint on the world scale destruction begins to produce order because the stable-constant of nothingness (or inactivity, a byproduct of destruction) outweighs that which is being destroyed.

While destroying only systems of order in which that left behind the pre-existing order might seem plausible, the only ways to circumvent this would be to create new chaos in the wake of destruction.

In this system destruction and entropy contributes to the final product, whereas stability and constancy are negated from the final product, therefore:

destruction + entropy - constancy – stability – inadvertent order = c & o scale product

If we assume 0 destruction on the perpetuate scale with entropy equal to ½ of total energy exerted, and temporarily minimize the negative effects of stability and constancy for the sake of simplicity, the phenomenon manifests graphically as follows:

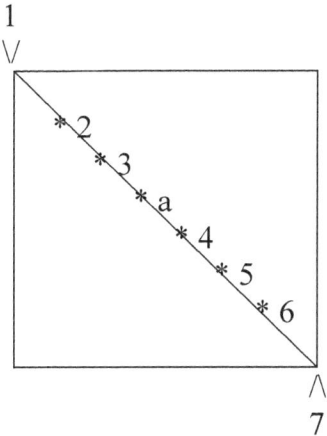

Fig. 21
System Scale

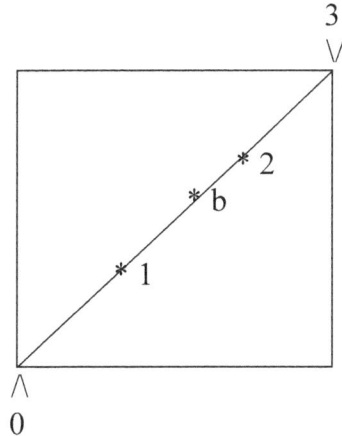

Fig. 22
System Perpetuate: Destruction

In Fig. 21 the order is at near maximum, represented by point 2. If the perpetuate scale (Fig.22) moves one increment, from point 0 to point 1, combined with the entropy equal to ½ the energy input, we would move 1.5 increments on the scale of chaos and order, represented by point a. This trend continues until the midpoint of the system perpetuate is reached, represented in Fig. 22 by "b." If the perpetuate scale continues any further the chaos and order scale will begin to shift back towards order. This is because the remnant of destruction is an order: either stable-constant, or nothingness. When destruction reaches half of its capacity, destroying anything more would leave a remnant of order greater than the amount of potential destruction which can occur. Order produced therefore, is equal to, or greater than the chaos produced after the system perpetuate destruction's midpoint. To circumvent this, the following is posited:

Creating New Chaos in the Wake of Destruction

For every increment of order produced after the perpetuate scale's midpoint, new subsystems of chaos must be created at a rate at which, when combined with entropy from the creation of order, they outweigh the order produced from the aftermath of destruction.

Destroying Order-Based Systems: Why it doesn't Work

At first glance destroying only order-based systems would seem the rational alternative to allowing a stable-constant order manifest via the destruction of aftermath. However, destroying order-based systems and replacing them with a single order—the aftermath of destruction—actually serves to increase the frequency at which order is created.

Total Destruction: The Final Solution

Though the stable-constant model is not the only model through which pure destruction can be achieved, for the sake of simplicity, the stable-constant model provides the best example.

Assuming that one implements the creation of distinctive chaotic systems, from the midpoint in Fig. 22, the scale can move to point 2 successfully, or, .5 increments from point "b." Therefore, after adding the effect of entropy, which we determined would be ½ of the energy input, we move one full increment on the system scale, ignoring the negative effects of stability and constancy for sake of simplicity[6]. If the system perpetuate moves another increment and distinctive chaotic systems are used to counterbalance the order generated from the aftermath of destruction the chaos and order scale will pursue its maximum output for chaos, represented by 7 in Fig. 21.

When the system scale reaches its maximum output and destruction has replaced a single order with many distinctive systems of chaos, we reach a state in which pure chaos = pure order. The autonomous system of distinctive orders, operates as a single system.

This is significant because, taking into consideration the ever-increasing level of entropy in the universe, reaching a state of pure destruction is one of the few, if not the only way, to achieve a state of pure order = pure chaos.

This is assuming that entropy, as well as entropic systems, cannot be reversed. The second law of thermodynamics states that the sum of

---

[6] It is possible that, even taking stability and constancy in effect, all phenomenon outlined in this section could still occur, therefore omitting the variables stability and constancy will only have the effect of simplifying the model, and making it easier to process.

entropy in isolated systems increases, leading to an increase in entropy on a universal scale. We will refer to this theory as **Universal Entropic Capacity**, whereas a less conventional hypothesis, that entropic systems can become kinetic if function of the system is changed, will be dubbed **Cyclic Entropy**. Infused with this latter theory is the concept that, at reaching a state of pure chaos = pure order, the entropic systems become functional in autonomy, thereby infusing the systems with energy to be used in new functions.

Universal Entropic Capacity

For the past twenty pages we've been referring to "system scale," which represents a system in which a change in chaos or order is occurring. The total sum of all worldly systems would result in the total composition of order and chaos in the world. The total sum of all systems in the universe would result in total composition of order and chaos in the universe. The scales through which the chaos composition of the world and universe are measured are referred to as the **world scale** and the **universal scale**. Both are system scales, but operate with lesser system scales in the manner that a system scale operates with the perpetuate. In ascending order, the perpetuate effects the system scale, which effects the world scale, and finally the universal scale.[7] To illustrate the effect of entropy in a state of pure order = pure chaos, we will look to the universal scale.

According to the 2nd? law of thermodynamics, the universe is becoming increasingly disordered due to entropic systems. This means that entropy will prevent the achievement of pure order by limiting the capacity of pure order.

---

[7] For more elaboration, consult the Hierarchy of Order-Based and Chaotic Systems on page 53.

Order
a
∨

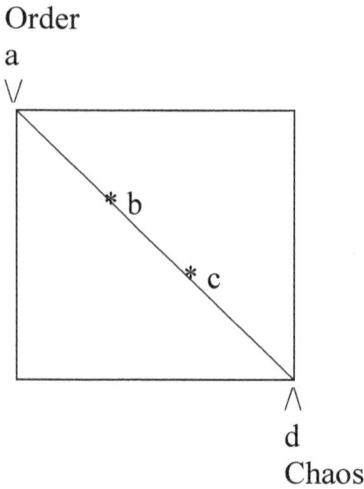

d
Chaos

Fig. 23

For example, Fig. 23 depicts a state of equilibrium (pure order=pure chaos) at the dawn of the universe, at which point no **cumulative entropy** existed. As soon as the first changes began to occur entropy was produced. As mentioned in prior sections, order produced can outweigh entropy. However, there is a limited capacity to which order can outweigh entropy.

The relationship between chaos and order is such that, pure order = pure chaos is a state of equilibrium. Pure chaos is an order in itself. It shares all the attributes of an order: it is consistent in its inconsistency, stable in its instability, predictable in its unpredictability. Chaos and order will always return to this state, but with diminishing return. The entropy produced will limit the capacity to which pure order can be achieved. Every time chaos and order return to the state of equilibrium via attaining pure order, following the first instance in which pure chaos = pure order, entropy will limit the capacity of order, and therefore the new equilibrium will be established at a new point known as **virtual equilibrium**.

If, for example, the world scale had moved from its initial point of equilibrium, and returned after a series of changes to a state of pure order the entropy produced would inhibit movement to the original capacity of order, represented by a in Fig. 15. Though the scale has reached pure order the full, original capacity of order has been lost partially, thus bringing the full capacity of order, or pure order, to increment b.

26

This phenomenon is especially important in justifying the only way in which pure order = pure chaos can be achieved, and that is by moving towards a state of pure chaos.

Calculating the Capacity of Order:

As stated in Chapter I, section 2, "Due to their dichotomous relationship in a system of limited capacity, such as one in which chaos and order can neither be created nor destroyed, only converted, when chaos goes up, order goes down. Models of this nature are considered closed models with a total value of 1." Therefore, mathematically determining the capacity of order is as simple as replacing the letters in prior figures with the respective numbers, associated with a closed system.

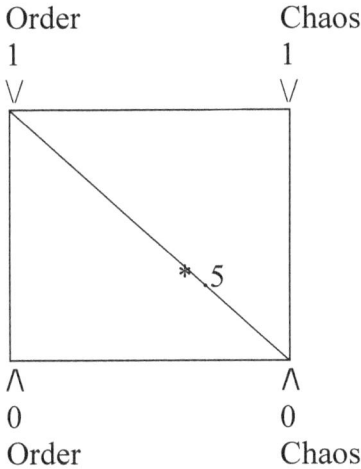

Order   Chaos
1   1
V   V

*.5

Λ   Λ
0   0
Order   Chaos

Fig. 24

We begin with the following equation:

(successful energy output + stability + constancy – entropy = product on c & o scale)

Let's start by assuming that the current balance between order and chaos lies below the midpoint in Fig 24, veering towards chaos. For the sake of accuracy assign order a current value of .3. A change is made, augmenting order's value to .5, and the equation above is used to calculate the

27

immediate value of the order produced. If the order produced outweighs the chaos and entropy then the capacity of order can be tested. Add the total value of entropy produced during the changes from the point of equilibrium to the point at which order reached its current position (.5 in this instance). Subtract total entropy from the full capacity (1), and the capacity at which order will reach its virtual state of equilibrium is established.

Of course, this method is somewhat erroneous due to the fact that you are calculating the capacity of order, assuming that no more entropy will be produced beyond that point. If the rate of entropy production is stable, then charting the final capacity of order is still relatively easy. Just calculate cumulative entropy of reaching your desired point. For example, say one wanted to reach .8 on the system scale in Fig. 16. At our current position of .5, we must move .3 increments. If entropy is being produced at a steady rate with a potency of ½ of energy input, then the .3 increments of movement will cause a 1.5 increment change in capacity of order.

If, with order at .5, entropy's current value was .15, and the .3 increment movement of order produced an additional .15, creating a total entropic value of .3, the value of order would not be allowed to exceed .7. Therefore, it is always a good idea to calculate the potential entropic value, and capacity of order. In this circumstance, a .3 change in value for order cannot occur because the capacity for order is 7. However, if order increases .2 increments from .5, producing a .05 increase in value for entropy, entropy's full value would be .2, leaving the potential capacity for order at .8. Continue calculating in this manner and you will find the midpoint at which entropy production and the entropic value will reach equilibrium. In this instance you would have to move just a little over half of one tenth of an increment (.065 perhaps) from .7, to generate .035 entropy and meet order's capacity with order totaling at or around .765 and entropy totaling .235. When their total value =1 the system's potential capacity of order has been established.

Adhering to the beliefs mentioned above requires taking into consideration the fact that, at some point cumulative entropy will reach a point at which the threshold of pure order will be achieved at the point of pure chaos.

Cyclical Entropy

In accordance with the belief that, were there a God he would have set the strings in motion and left us to the folly of his system, is the theory of cyclic entropy. Cyclic entropy postulates that the universal system of chaos and order fluctuates between two states of equilibrium, one achieved through pursuit of order and the other through degradation of order and increasing entropic value, which results in pure chaos = pure order. At this point entropic systems become a part of the new autonomous order. The systems' function may change, resulting in release of potential energy, once assumed irreversible.

For example, imagine two tubs of water, one hot and one cold. When these two tubs of water reach their state of equilibrium the system has released all potential energy and has consequently become entropic. Though the system itself is entropic, taking the once hot tub of water, now room temperature, and placing it at odds with a tub of cold water will allow an additional release of energy. Continue this process until the original hot tub of water is cold. Do likewise with the once cold tub of water until it becomes hot. Now, when placed at odds with a hot tub of water, the original system occurs again. The example illustrates how entropic systems can be "recharged," not reversed.

An additional example of an entropic system is the mixing of dye and water. Once dye and water reach a state of equilibrium their work against the grain of the other is complete, the system is complete, energy spent, and system irreversible. Take the dye and water solution, mix it with a liquid more or less dense, and watch the entropic water-dye system become the perpetuate of new, organized work in a new system. A substance which, when immersed in a new system, can still perform work has yet to reach a state of **absolute entropy**, a state in which a substance reaches its simplest form, and can perform the minimal amount of work, if any at all.

As for a system being irreversible, everything in the universe distinguishable by man differs in function and workability. While water and dye are mixed it is possible that, upon entering new systems in which work can still be performed, there will be a point at which the different nature of dye molecules and water molecules cause them to perform work differently, and perhaps strip the two elements from one another's bond once more.

The point is that all things are in a constant state of interaction with different systems, and that essentially due to this, all functions, depending on exposure to differing systems, are subject to change. Essentially, all systems and components are in a perpetual state of reorganization, not increased disorder.

On the universal scale it means this: order and chaos reconstitute themselves as one another at the point at which pure order = pure chaos. Just as the hot and cold tubs of water, chaos perpetuated by destruction can become order, order perpetuated by creation can become chaos, functions and states change, reorganize, and overall, the universal system mimics the pendulum swing, fluctuating between pursuit of equilibrium through order, then through chaos, a virtual "cleansing" of entropy is underwent at the point where pure order = pure chaos, and the system begins once more.

Denominations

Both of the above theories have their validity and shortcomings. Cyclic entropy, for example, fixes itself in the hypothetical, and in some cases unproven phenomenon. Both are synonymous in that they retain the idea that true equilibrium comes at the point at which pure chaos = pure order, but both achieve this point by very different means.

Due to these distinctions there are two denominations, or conglomerates of sub-groups who advocate for their respective system. Any advocates of free will likely believe in entropic capacity, for it implies there is not a stable system through which our universe reaches an equilibrium. Rather, it is a sum of the systems, some dictated by chance, some by will, which determine the outcome of the world. Most anarchists believe in entropic capacity because they believe free will is the true perpetuate of anarchy.

Advocates of Cyclic entropy include neo-anarchists. The neo-anarchist realizes that the universe is a perpetual pendulum set into motion eons ago. Since that point, we have bounced between the equilibriums, giving rebirth to order through chaos. The neo-anarchist realizes that autonomy is dictated by the initial changes in the universe, and that everything is a reaction spawned from the initial moment, and that there is truly no free will, only the will of autonomy.

Stable-Inconstant: Chaos

In this system destruction, inconstancy, and entropy contribute to the final product, whereas stability is negated from the final product, therefore:

$$destruction + entropy + inconstancy - stability - inadvertent\ order = c\ \&\ o\ scale\ product$$

A fairly comfortable environment for order, the stable-inconstant model also provides the potential for growth to chaos. Consult Fig. 16 for graphical depiction, and the section titled "Stable-Inconstant: Order" for a more acute description of the system variables.

Chapter IV: Unstable Change

Unstable-Constant: Order-Based

Fig. 17 depicts the first possible unstable-constant system of change we will discuss. If we use creation in this model to perpetuate order then we have the successful energy output, and the constancy of the system to counterbalance the instability and the resultant entropy. Therefore:

successful energy output + constancy – entropy + instability – inadvertent chaos = product on c & o scale

Creating Water or Destroying Ice: Practical Application of the Order-Based Unstable-Constant Model

As stated previously, Fig. 17 depicts the unstable-constant system of change. The figure has been reproduced below:

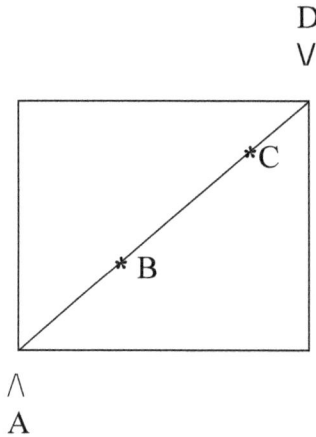

Fig. 25
Unstable-Constant

While the distances from point A to B and from point B to C are relatively equal. The distance from point C to maximum output is minimal.

In this example we are dealing with the means by which the perpetuate moves towards the final outcome, which in this example's case is order via creation of water, or, destruction of ice and water. In this instance the means is altered by man, and instability occurs as a result of man's choice of timing. This model is purely hypothetical, and could as easily be stable due to man's choice of time he wishes to expose the ice to each means.

From point A to point B light affects the ice cube. In revolution two, from point B to point C, salt affects the ice cube. Finally, from point C to point D the remaining ice and water is exposed to heat.

The nature of the experiment is such that the perpetuate, while constantly moving the system scale towards final output, is doing so at different intervals of time per revolution, thus creating an unstable-constant system.

Now, imagine if we changed the active perpetuate from creation of evaporation to destruction of ice. The rate of instability and constancy remains the same, but stability and efficiency of each means improves. For example, salt is more effective at destroying ice than creating water. The same may be said for heat for it is as likely to evaporate water as destroy the ice.

If the variable of stability were not affected by man in this model then the level of instability would change as well. Say for example, that each heat, salt, and light were used to destroy ice and comparatively create water. Salt, in this instance, would not only be more efficient at destroying ice than creating water, it would destroy ice at a faster rate than creating water, therefore changing the level of stability over the course of a three-stage system.

Unstable-Constant: Chaos-Based

Fig. 25 serves to illustrate the nature of destruction in the unstable constant model. If we use destruction in this model then we have the only the constancy of the system weighing against the desired final output, the instability and the resultant entropy. Therefore:

(Instability + entropy + chaos produced – constancy = result)

While in the last paradigm we were attempting to create water, in this paradigm we are attempting to destroy ice. While all three methods of conversion are effective at both creating water and destroying ice, thus resulting in an equal constancy, each has a different level of efficiency. For example, salt is much more efficient when destroying ice than when creating water. Heat likely has an equilibrium temperature at which ice is destroyed and water created at an equal rate. But ultimately, due to the variable temperature heat has a variable relationship with the object it performs work on in any form of conversion.

As a result, the level and rate of instability will vary between the same model when viewed through the lens of destruction, and then again under the lens of creation, which is why it is essential this distinction in the processes of conversion be made, as rates of efficiency and stability are variable depending on the perpetuate through which they are observed.

Unstable-Inconstant: Order-Based

Order is rarely generated, if ever, in such a system.

Instability + inconstancy + entropy – order generated — inadvert chaos = product

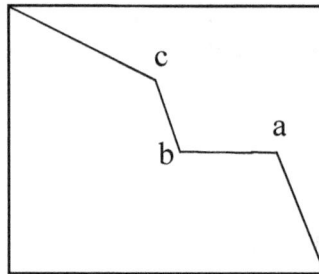

Fig. 26
Unstable-Inconstant

Fig. 26 represents the graphical depiction of the unstable-inconstant model. This model is characterized by unsteady incremental growth heading in sporadic inconstant directions.

34

A natural system in which the unstable inconstant model applies is that of water retention, or, conversion from ice and evaporated water to water, or in our case the creation of water. While the graph above does not correspond precisely with the natural system of conversions to water it does serve to illustrate the basic trends over the time frame of three seasons starting with spring and ending with fall.

Through the time-frame of a four season model the conversion of evaporated water and ice to water follows an unstable-inconstant pattern, which achieves only relative constancy and stability. From the starting point to point a, we have a large amount of conversion from ice to water due to the onset of spring. But from point a to point b, the water freezes again, causing some of the water to be lost, thus establishing inconstancy. The instability is the result of temperature variables, and the time that these temperatures remain a part of the four season system. Imagine that the short incremental growth between a and b is representative of conversion in temperatures barely below freezing. The model illustrates how this would result in a less effective reversal of conversion to water. The short period of time the freezing temperatures were predominant, combined with the inefficiency of the conversion results in a small revolution and, relative to the growth rate of surrounding revolutions, creates the unstable environment.

The large incremental growth between the starting point and point a, caused by a relatively moderate temperature, results in increased melting and minimal evaporation.

The remainder of the model would follow suit, with the increase in conversion to water from points b to c illustrating a return to spring, c to d illustrating a short summer in which evaporation outweighs water which has melted, and d to e illustrating the rain and prelude to autumn.

Unstable-Inconstant: Chaos

(Instability + inconstancy + entropy + chaos produced = result)

Note that this is the only model formula in which all factors positively contribute to the outcome. Considering the high likelihood that universal entropic capacity exists, this is also the only model through which a state of equilibrium, i.e. pure order=pure chaos can be achieved.

Once we begin to progress towards a state in which entropy has begun to accumulate, and only virtual equilibrium can be feasibly achieved it is very difficult to return to a state of pure order.

There are three posited ways reaching a state of pure order can be achieved once cumulative entropy enters the picture:

1. Assimilate pre-existing orders into a single order.
2. Destroy everything
3. Progress towards a state of autonomy via isolating all systems, or, "destroying" connectives within a single order, or by destroying pre-existing orders and replacing them with chaos.

The first option fails to take into consideration the very problem of cumulative entropy, totally disregarding the fact that unless the single order is the full capacity of cumulative entropy itself then cumulative entropy will always inhibit a single order from reaching its maximum universal potential. Reaching the full capacity of entropy, however, is another means to reaching the state of pure order = pure chaos. The entropy's capacity becomes an autonomous universal system, thus a single order all under the same law: autonomy.

The second possibility is feasible, but the problem of non-existence comes into play. When all is destroyed, is complete destruction an order due to the fact that it results in the most potent expression of stability: inactivity, or is complete destruction an order due to the non-existence of all distinctions and delineations? Likely both. In the extreme sense of the latter, what if nothing at all exists as a result of universal destruction? Can such a phenomenon truly be considered an order of non-existence? If nothing is occurring over infinite time then we would seem to have succeeded in creating a single order, or state of equilibrium, with all, or rather, nothing, dictated by one law: inactivity.

The third is the most feasible, as the first requires universal entropic capacity to occur, which requires that this third and final means to creating a state of equilibrium to occur several times over. Each time we destroy orders and replace them to the point that we reach equilibrium we come closer to reaching universal entropic capacity. The quickest way to achieve the desirable system state at which pure chaos = pure order, therefore, is to destroy orders and replace them with distinctive systems in which all working aspects of the order become their own system, and individualized autonomy occurs.

36

Glossary of Terms

Absolute Entropy: A substance which, when immersed in a new system, can still perform work, has yet to reach a state of **absolute entropy**, a state in which a substance reaches its simplest form, and can perform the minimal amount of work, if any at all.

Anarchy: Similar to, and the father of, neo-anarchy. The most significant difference between the anarchist and the neo-anarchist is that the anarchist sees autonomy as an ends, whereas the neo-anarchist sees autonomy as a rebirth, and a means to establishing a new order.

Catalysis: The process by which a perpetuate changes, and in turn changes the balance of chaos and order on the world scale. If a perpetuate has a positive effect on the final intended outcome, it is a catalyst.

Change: The incremental progress of any given system over a given course of time is known as change.

Change-Stage: Generally synonymous with a system-scale. However, there are times when measurement of a system over an extended period of time will feature several change-stages. For example, in the process of converting ice to water, a change-stage is synonymous with a system-scale. However, when converting ice to steam, there are two change-stages within the system scale, which measures the entire process of conversion.

Chaos: A universal factor independent of good and evil, which, in coordination with order, determines the total capacity of any given system. Chaos is a variable response or byproduct of any of the three perpetuates.

Constancy: The persistence towards a given direction over a fixed period of time.

Controlled Chaos: A lotto machine shoots random balls into a machine. Though the ball is random, the fact that "a ball" is entering the machine makes the phenomenon a controlled chaos.

Cumulative Entropy: Entropy that accumulates on the universal scale, and limits the successive points at which the world scale reaches equilibrium in that cumulative entropy lowers the maximum output for order on the world scale. Cumulative entropy would eventually lead to a maximum output of 0 for order on the world scale, unless there was a means of 'recycling' entropy, such as when pure chaos, partially composed of entropy, = pure order.

Destruction: One of the three perpetuates. Destruction is generally a means of producing chaos, but in particular circumstances, it is quite a potent force when positively affecting order as well. Such as when destruction on the world scale reaches the midpoint, and more order is generated from destruction than chaos during, and as a result of destruction.

Entropy: is a primary variable in determining the effect of a system perpetuate on the chaos and order scale. This is because entropy contributes to the increase of disorder in the universe, a state which is believed to be irreversible. Entropy in itself represents the degradation of energy from a productive state to non-productive.

Entropic Threshold: When the entropy from a number of systems in any environment fully inhibits the natural flow of energy towards a state of equilibrium in a subsequent system.

Energy: The essence that fuels work of any system in the universe. There are several different forms of energy: heat energy, electrical energy, kinetic energy, potential energy, radiant energy, chemical energy and atomic energy. Force x Distance = work. Force x Distance \ Time = Rate of work. In a change-stage, measure the rate of work in each revolution and subtract the result of each revolution from the preceding revolution to determine the rate of stability. To determine the rate of constancy in a change-stage, divide the product of work of each revolution by the incremental growth of each revolution and subtract the difference in incremental growth of a revolution from the preceding revolution.

Incremental Change: For natural systems, the incremental change is determined by the number of revolutions which occur within a given change-stage. If there are twelve revolutions in a system of 60 minutes, then we have twelve increments of change. From this we can determine the rate of change.

Inhibition: The process by which a perpetuate changes, and in turn changes the balance of chaos and order on the world scale. If a perpetuate has a negative effect on the final intended outcome, it is known as an inhibitor.

Neo-Anarchy: Whether by means of perpetuating distinctive orders, or chaos, or by being justice seeker, or evildoer, the neo-anarchist looks to reach and preserve the state of autonomy, and supports the continuation of the unstable-inconstant system to reach autonomy.

Perceptual Chaos: Each individual has a perceptual capacity, which is synonymous with a sensory threshold, at which point an individual becomes over stimulated, cannot put order to the things around them, and thus is immersed in perceptual chaos. Each sense has an independent threshold. When two or more senses are stimulated simultaneously there is a collective threshold as well. The collective threshold limits the independent threshold of each sense to a greater degree for each sense simultaneously stimulated.

Perpetuate: The perpetuate, and the perpetuate scale, measures the amount of change caused by one of the catalysis. The three perpetuates are creation, destruction, and conversion. Changes on the perpetuate scale generally reflect proportionally relevant changes on the other scales of the hierarchy.

Primary Perpetuate: The primary perpetuate is a perpetuate which works independently in a system.

Rate of Change: To determine the rate of change, one must take the total incremental growth of a system, and the total time in which it took the system to reach final output. Divide total incremental growth by total time. For example, say that 2 increments of growth had occurred over the course of 20 minutes. When we divide the incremental growth (2) by the time (20 min) we get .1 increments per minute. One can also calculate rate of change for any given measurement of time within a closed system: per hour, per second, per millisecond, etc.

Relative Constancy: Phenomenon occurring when an inconstant pattern continues to repeat itself over a series of changes measured together.

Relative Stability: Phenomenon occurring when an unstable pattern continues to repeat itself over a series of changes measured together.

Revolution: A revolution occurs within a system scale. Represented in the system scale, a revolution is most easily recognized as the small intervals which chart the level of stability in a system. These intervals represent fluctuations in rate of change, or process on the system scale. For example, when ice is converted into steam, two full change-stages occur: the conversion from ice to water, and the conversion from water to steam. During each change-stage, fluctuations in efficiency occur. These fluctuations are revolutions. To measure stability in a system where only one revolution occurs, calculate rate of change from beginning of process to the middle, and from middle to end. Calculate rate of change per 10 second interval for a more accurate and detailed reading of stability.

Secondary Perpetuate: Secondary perpetuates hinge upon, or are impacted by, the work of another perpetuate in a given system.

Stable-Constant: Any system characterized by both a stable rate of change, and a constant incremental growth towards a particular output, is known as a stable-constant system.

Stability: The rate of incremental change that occurs over a fixed period of time, in which each change-stage takes the same amount of time to complete.

System Stability: Term coined to distinguish chaos theory stability from kinetic stability and thermodynamic stability. See **Stability**

Time-Change: Constancy is measured in terms of incremental change. Stability is measured in terms of time-change.

Unstable Constant: A system characterized by unstable rate of change and a constant incremental growth towards a particular output, is known as an unstable-constant system.

Universal or Natural Chaos: Universal chaos, represented by the universal scale, is the total amount of chaos derived from all systems in the universe.

Universal Scale: The total sum of all systems in the universe graphically depicted. The Universal scale is preceded by the world scale.

Value: is measured in terms of the amount of deviation relative to the amount of revolutions which have occurred.

Virtual Equilibrium: The point at which pure chaos = pure order on the world scale, as the capacity of both has been simultaneously achieved, but order is stifled due to the accumulation of entropy on the universal scale.

World Scale: The total sum of all worldly systems graphically depicted. The world scale precedes the universal scale, and follows the independent system scales representing the divers systems on earth.

Index of Relevant Laws, Scientific and Non-scientific:

The Law of Diminishing Returns: The law of diminishing returns states that since the dawn of time, and the inception of equilibrium, all change has produced entropy, thus limiting order's maximum capacity. The entropy produced from each system is order which can never be re-established, therefore the original maximum capacity becomes replaced by a virtual capacity.

1st Law of Thermodynamics: The first law of thermodynamics describes both the Law of Conservation of Energy: which states that energy can neither be created nor destroyed, and the Law of Conservation of Mass: which states that energy can neither be created nor destroyed.

2nd law of Thermodynamics: The sum of entropy in isolated systems increases, leading to an increase in entropy on a universal scale.

Hierarchy of Order-Based and Chaotic Systems:

For mankind, there is relative motion. We sit still, but the world revolves. Independent systems in the world are in a state of relative stillness, while on the world scale we are all in relative motion. These distinctions make it necessary to isolate systems at any level they operate. Within the system model there are distinctive levels at which one can measure change:

1. molecular change
2. atomic change
3. chemical change

The changes within any interwoven individual systems is measured on the system scale. The compilation of all worldly systems is measured on the world scale.

The Forms of Change

Incremental change – refers to constancy

Time-change – refers to stability

Both time-change and incremental change can be applied to any scale, world, universal, stage, revolution, etc. Below are the various stages or scales, in ascending order.

The Hierarchy

I. Revolution

A *revolution* is measured in isolation on the "revolution scale". Revolutions occur within a stage-change or, system-change.

II. Stage-Change

A stage-change is generally synonymous with system-change. However, there are circumstances in which several change-stages occur within a system. This circumstance is relative to measurement. See definition for further clarification.

III. The Perpetuate

The perpetuate is measured in isolation on perpetuate scale. There are three perpetuates: destruction, creation, and conversion. Essentially all perpetuates are forms of conversion.

IV. System-change

A system change is measured in isolation, on the system scale. Revolutions occur within the system scale.

V. World change

World change is measured in isolation on the world scale. All independent systems in the world compile to create the composition of chaos and order on the world scale.

VI. Universal change

Universal change is measured in isolation on the universal scale. All world systems and other universal phenomenon compile to create the composition of chaos and order on the universal scale.

Contact Information:

If you are interested in acquiring further information on the works of Henry Kirchhoff or Psychoplasmic Pulp Publishing, please contact us:

psychoplasmicpulppress@gmail.com

www.ingramcontent.com/pod-product-compliance
Lightning Source LLC
Chambersburg PA
CBHW060544030426
42337CB00021B/4426